SOME GIRLS

WALK INTO

THE COUNTRY

THEY ARE

FROM

SOME GIRLS

WALK

INTO   SAWAKO NAKAYASU

THE COUNTRY

THEY   ARE FROM

WAVE BOOKS   SEATTLE

AND   NEW YORK

Published by Wave Books

www.wavepoetry.com

Copyright © 2020 by Sawako Nakayasu

All rights reserved

Wave Books titles are distributed to the trade by

Consortium Book Sales and Distribution

Phone: 800-283-3572 / SAN 631-760X

Library of Congress Cataloging-in-Publication Data

Names: Nakayasu, Sawako, 1975- author. | Nakayasu, Sawako, 1975-

 Poems. Selections | Nakayasu, Sawako, 1975- Poems. Selections. French. |

 Nakayasu, Sawako, 1975- Poems. Selections. Japanese.

Title: Some girls walk into the country they are from / Sawako Nakayasu

Description: First edition. | Seattle : Wave Books, [2020].

Identifiers: LCCN 2020015633 | ISBN 9781950268122 (hardcover) |

 ISBN 9781950268115 (paperback)

Classification: LCC PS3614.A575 A1995 2020 | DDC 811/.6—dc23

LC record available at https://lccn.loc.gov/2020015633

Designed by Crisis

Printed in the United States of America

9 8 7 6 5 4 3 2 1

First Edition

Wave Books 088

GENÈVE CHAO

LYNN XU

HITOMI YOSHIO

KYONGMI PARK

KYOKO YOSHIDA

KAREN AN-HWEI LEE

MIWAKO OZAWA

FOR

EUGENE KANG

CONTENTS

SOME

GIRLS WALK

INTO THE

COUNTRY   THEY

ARE

FROM

GIRLS ROLLING THEMSELVES

There is a symptom in the proposition when that abundance gangs up,
head cocks to the heat bending towards both livable and untenable,
the exit grows and grows forgetful of its nature as orifice, hand
slackens in relation, a wrestle of train car, company, one day as if
any other day, or night. Send me their off.

Something uncanny about these girls. Something believing and barely
visible. I din, in vain. Breath, too full. Persist, hinder, say too much,
as if it were Vegas.

Some get the stars shaken off of them. Some are given rose-scent.
Some are fed animal protein to fatten them up for the flood.

When they emerge, they are ten new girls, A through J.

GIRLS INHABIT ARCH

One girl's lips tremble mountainous. One fears the loss of delicate facts. One slides right off. One leaves a fingerprint in my eye.

Here is what I know for sure.

One girl is a gift. One girl is a city. One girl is a city visiting another city not itself. One girl is sadness. One girl is a well.

The hat styled with pigeon wings is not a girl. I've told you this before. The girl walking nonchalantly through the streets of a European city is not a girl, unless there is a bat. The girl too full of walks, of women, of sights, comes to pause under the arch.

I mix think female all the time. I shook-hot your fat into mine. I arch you to the tender touch, that was a burn. I statue my limits into a marble female gaze. That is to say, I am looking at you. You look for a door. We are outside. O, we are out.

TEM GIRLS IN THE OPEM ROOM

That old play. One tomgue deep in the woumd.

One breaks off and heads northdrifter. One simks well I guess imto
the floor. One accepts a fake comfirmation that the room is still
opem. Sevem left eventually fading their rights away.

All tem bretty okay with none of it pretty tope. No one said
couldbye. Same den bold the gorner and observe attempted rescue.
Some of the tem pend at the torso then squat, emerge. The excess of
what flows is never silemt.

One tonne dear to my world.

Then disbamd, as soom as the room is opem. Side loom of the mind. I
loll back the missingness for the sake of a roll of grief. Complicated
dirt floods my kidney—those stars crisp outlines, stone falls out a
wilting body, cusp of absemce like somme other.

UNDER THE CONDITION OF SENDING A WARM THING BY SPOON

When asked who wants to ride, sometimes the girls jump up and down, othertimes they duck, cover, and conceal. In the beginning it was Girl D, Girl E, Girl G, Girl H, Girl I, and Girl J. The girls who are not yet moms but want that ride have been carting their potential children in a pouch somewhere. When Girl J marries a gay man, he repeatedly says, I'm gay, you know I'm gay, right? Girl J says of course, don't forget all the times I've been cruising with you. And there goes the warm thing. Will you be my spoon, forever and ever.

NOW THE BRIDGE A GREY ORCHID

Belonging to Girl H, designated at birth. Over time evolved from
今　さら屋根　やら橋　やら灰色　の蘭　とか言われ　ても黒い idea of
orchid 絵 to image of orchid to real orchid, described as fitting for
Girl H—how perfect, how complimentary, how beautiful.

We do not draw attention to the fact that they have long ceased
to mention のなか　でうご　めいてい　る濃い色の　花が武　器だと
Girl H and her grey orchid. In fact all of this took place so long ago
that Girl H's understanding of the orchid is limited to the vague
いうこ　とだけ　は隠し sensation of a residual history.

At the great bridge Girl H is asked to present her papers. All she 通し
has is the grey orchid. They accept it, but not without reminding her
that she is crossing with a bad orchid. They will be checking on her
て行こう. Her foot falters; she crosses. In the distance, a field of
daisies waving.

DIX FILLES DANS UN PAQUET DE CHIPS

Se battent pour le droit de choisir son chip comme s'il n'y avait que dix chips dans le paquet. Il y a plus de dix chips dans le paquet.

Fille A présuppose que plus c'est gros, plus c'est rond, mieux c'est. Fille G croit que les plus belles devraient avoir le droit de choisir en premier. Fille C tente d'avancer la règle de la capacité pulmonaire totale. Fille J voit que les chips en forme de lame pourraient un jour être utiles. Elle reste silencieuse. Fille I refuse.

Seule Fille H note que tout reste si croustillant que le récipient, je veux dire le sachet, où elles demeurent doit être fermé. Seule Fille H ait un sens de sa vraie situation dans l'économie globale et la chaîne logistique alimentaire et de comment cela va changer le sort à toutes. Elle a du mal à décider entre parler, gifler, ou rester muette.

GIRLS STEALING THE AIR
OUT OF MY BULMONES

Pald girls and old girls and nonpald girls and marapona folded girls, all
of them show me the ubside of t'espoir by arriving at my bulmonary
entrée with their individual air hags pillowing in my quickening intake,
drop um by um into my panier of helupu is on the way, a way, a gut
slap tarte out of here, instructions gesture towards memory, all balled
up and thing-like, fall play to landing on thickets of interior lushlush &
quiet tumble rush upwards

a path
opening elsewhere a newer purchase on my little paggie of emergency
air, fleshfleshiness of lung matter thereby under the premise that it
can be given back, theft flies temporarily so, dake it given it back, I
bold out, I open, I close, trying to trap a girl in the fact you make me
peel like a natural erreur force of artifice admonished absorption, now
witness that, holdholt it open again, orbiting again, new definitions
of ownership, felt presence of taking it, don't don't you dank it now.

GIRL F OR GIRL I OR GIRL J IN A CUP, IN A BATTERY, IN A SHEET OF PAPER AT A POINT WHEN IT CEASES TO HOLD

The business of the hand supports the claims of the trench. Spatial folds of time swell and ripen, broke oft open. Having been overwhelming, sensation of falling over and over across the fold and beyond the rim, exposed to a blunt give. Girl who keeps to the inside of the circular stone of the cup, battery, and sheet. Keep running within or spill out. F, I, or J. It wasn't a girl in the first place, not like that, and what a horrible pit, lie against joy. Paper and batteries in a cup. F and I, don't mine me. Gull, Garuru, and "Girl" are pieces of the table swept slowly by the arm, and all that remains after all that which glows.

GIRLS RESPOND QUICKLY
TO A CALL FROM HIGH UP

It was summer and we had stopped to see the Tule Tree on the
grounds of the church in Santa María. I was twenty-five at the time
and I had twenty-five daughters, one for every year of my birth.
I was carrying all of them, one on top of another, and my mother,
too, I was carrying, and one by one they were climbing into the
canopy of the ahuehuete. Aie. Aie. Aie. Society is grotesque and
proliferates in broad daylight, but there is time within time and
adolescence still waiting.

IS IT SAFE FOR GIRLS TO
HAVE FAVORITE BEARS

Midsummer night fires inelegant displays of annihilation.

From the thick strident part of a curvature, Girl G trespasses in the lesser passions. An amange, convaincted and groaling, originates possible viscosities into a torrent of escape, advances a graceful, probing exit.

Girl B on one small ride of light, I know it like the back of my wrist. The woke sunset is a painting. When I look too closely, I am flicked and whistled away by a distant cousin of civility.

WHEN GIRL B ROLLS OVER AND QUANTIFIES IT ALL OVER AGAIN

A matter of not having waited for this. Angle of forearm, love versus KO'd by love.

Despite measures checks trappings securities.

How many hours until it blows over this time. Ease of being strange, my wound of strange return.

Forty-five degrees Celsius. Minus twenty-five degrees Celsius. How much for this bottle of shimmer. Belly of the leg. Torque, as mere substitute.

De light. Developed in. No longer my fight to flee.

A LINE OF FIVE GIRLS WITH GOLFBALLS IN THEIR MOUTHS

Meets a line of five girls with tennisballs in their mouths

In front of a line of five girls with basketballs under their shirts.

At any given moment, the tennisball girls are directly in front of the basketball girls, perfectly in sync. In fact, it is absolutely imperative that the basketball girls do not reveal their basketballs under any circumstances. Everything is fine with this unique and slightly more athletic version of country line dancing—that is, until the whole grid of dancing girls ends up dancing their way onto the fairway, right in the middle of the US Open. With their left thumbs still hooked in the pockets of their cowboy jeans, each girl uses their right hand to pull out a baggie of invisibility powder, rhythmically shaking it all over themselves until there is nothing left to see except for beautifully fine residual vectors, the fine-tuned lines that they are. With these new and beautiful vectors, as well as the golfballs in the mouths of the five girls with golfballs in their mouths, they proceed to intervene in the outcome of the major golf tournament. Followed by the US Open in tennis. When the grid of girls makes it all the way to Madison Square Garden, they start dropping babies all over that basketball court as if the world was on fire and they needed to drop some weight so they could mad dash their way out of there. Basketballs, I mean.

GIRL SOUP

I get tired of being the one to make all the decisions so when they ask me where I want to eat, I say that I don't care, I'd eat anything at this point. Next thing I know, I am face-to-face with a bowl of Girl Soup and I just can't bring myself. Some of us at the table are in a hurry to eat the soup, they are specifically trying to eat the girls quickly because they seem to know that if you wait too long they turn into cyborgs or robots, and those are harder to chew. I can see that some of the girls are still alive and perhaps would like to be extracted from the soup, but when I squint I see that there are girls all over the floor with varying amounts of soup clinging to their clothes (you didn't think they were naked, did you?) and so there goes that idea. Just at the moment I think I have run out of options, something comes over me and I take a deep breath and I do it, I jump right in there, that bowl of Girl Soup, no one is checking IDs or questioning my size or gender or race or voter affiliation, and I quick round up all the girls in the bowl into a large huddle. We have now obliterated two major problems: huddled together we are too large to eat, and also we've taken care of the problem of the eater.

TEN MASTURBATING GIRLS UTOPIA

Here and not here and at the same time all at the same but not
same place or only if you count a few pows. As wives have pows too.
Having recently escaped the City of the Captive Element. Having
absolute and wavy belief in their hum, right, tsk, risk of arrival.
Here or rather now more than ten girls. A well-designed moment has
backups for every girl. No moment without please pleasure, marble
you out, heavily polished hammer, delicate flowers lined up all lined
up on the sidelines, cheer.

I defend these girls but only in this voicing, as soon as I count to
ten they have scattered their heavy wares and have nothing left to
lose but their bodies great bodies I step out so as to allow them to
continue their noumenal turn. In the capital of each body is a glint,
they limn it. I lose the line. All ten girls go like this:

[Sing]

Later they sidestepped, they hammered, they buckled, swung sallow,
wandered dreamy. They wilderness ran lightly, they lit it.

Commend the fanciness of these vulgar girls but only in this event. As soon as they have placed, I regret carrying their loving moonbreeze decadence with me. I have no reference left to blow, their failures great failures I clarify and let go. I mean it ongoing a neutral turn. In the job of the girl, winning to be. All girls then and their overlapping shimmer.

COUCH

Mai soofut lilt tendr, too laite, tullaide, bhrootl in laitened yoll. Or
booth. A baith on the tella colla, colnering, brikik a plasik. Hwere
in the brackish braike. Ek'sting, wishtng funk all, ai giff it all yuice,
ivry theng eny wing. Ai um capp't and aizy ulle dai lung. Ai fillut,
wi-marrut, braike—mar'agin. Ai a tree, you ekstick lute, ai ritern ta
crai und yu hud khald it. Tu egs en the fraing pann. Ivry theng on
urdur, furnich, hir. Heet t'swifft, pop.

QUEL DRÔLE DE PAYS

Filles A à J sont dans un nouveau pays. En tant que bonnes et sérieuses invitées, elles font comme les gens du pays. Faut être poli. Donc quand Fille A vomit, Fille B tend ses deux mains pour l'attraper, car dans ce nouveau pays il ne faut absolument pas que le vomi touche la terre. Fille B passe ensuite le vomi dans les mains en coupe de Fille C, qui le passe dans les mains en coupe de Fille D. Et ainsi de suite. Les mains des filles qui l'ont déjà passé sont recouvertes d'une fine couche de vomi. Elles attendent patiemment que ça sèche—elles n'ont pas le droit de se laver les mains.

Ça passe en rond, ce vomi, jusqu'à ce qu'il n'en reste plus suffisamment pour passer. Les filles se déplacent alors dans un endroit avec davantage de soleil pour accélérer le séchage de la couche de vomi sur les mains. Puis, enfin, elles passent à autre chose.

Fille E retourne dans sa tête les événements de ce nouveau pays lorsqu'une informatrice locale lui chuchote à l'oreille. Ce qu'elle entend faillit lui faire vomir, à Fille E, elle le goûte au fond de la gorge, mais elle avale fort et parvient à se retenir.

GIRL H FINALLY SAYS FUCK THAT SHIT AND JUMPS INTO MY POCKET

The little pocket on the left side of my chest, she settles in all cozy like a cartoon mouse. She says she is done with humans. Rather than take any further action, she now sends little kicks through my shirt so that I can behave accordingly on both her and my behalf.

One kick means go, two is yes. Three, four, and five kicks are for how many beats to wait before making a move. Six: breathe. And one more: let go of that scowl. Seven quick ones tickle me out of an awkward situation; this can create a nervous laughter that gets me in trouble and I start wondering if Girl H is really on my side or not. Eight: stop. Nine kicks in bursts of three are a modified SOS, and I need to stop and attend to whatever is going on inside that pocket, like something I said could have made her shit her pants right there on my chest, at which point I would need to excuse myself to take care of it as quickly as I possibly can.

And so it goes. There is one more I will never reveal: one hundred. By the time Girl H goes there, I know that I am done for. Her tiny foot beating on my chest slowly replaces my own heartbeat, it's an unconventional way to do things but that's it for me, I can see the long-haul truck approaching from a distance, look down and see my own feet planted in the wildest of grasses, lush, reaching, lineal, she is already in me, not just in my pocket, but that beat is no longer breath, nor direction—it just is, and is, and is, the bullshit meter breaks itself and jumps out the window, I breathe and breathe and breathe until I let go and it all grows very quiet for a while.

GIRL B HAS BROUGHT A
GIANT SHEET WITH THEM

While everyone else is busy crying over a communal loss of innocence, only Girl B is quietly at work, digging with their bare hands, gathering. From here it looks like dirt and from there it also looks like dirt, but from beneath the pile, from underneath the stuff that looks like dirt, it is the stuff that is getting away, that is what separates the stuff that looks like dirt from the stuff that also looks like dirt but is in fact the stuff that is getting away, fundamentally altering the nature of its existence. The stuff that clings to the loose gathering of their fingers, the stuff that doesn't fall through, not before holding on just long enough to land somewhere within the bounds of the giant sheet, I said giant but really it is just big enough to seat one regular-sized adult, but today there is no sitting on that sheet, that space is reserved for some very important dirt. It is the dirt that is going, going with Girl B.

When Girl B has accrued enough dirt, they bundle up their sheet, politely say goodbye, and begin the difficult part of the story. Everyone else busy crying over less significant matters, the afternoon light shines softly upon the back of Girl B, who walks alone. At the border they hold tight. At the crossing they hold tight. At the bridge they hold tight, unfazed by the sudden wind. At the horizon they hold tight for as long as they can manage, continue to move steadily forward while gripping as tightly as they possibly can, for they are too vividly aware that once it breaks loose, their hold on the sheet, there is no use trying to contain that dirt and they won't even try, it is really all that clear as night for everyone inside them to see.

THE COLOR OF GIRL E'S FACE
AS I BREAK THE NEWS TO HER

Is not the same as the way I looked when you caught me in a lie, it
was supposed to be tiny and harmless but I couldn't help the way it
spread across my face and beyond its edges and through the airspace
to land and expand thickly on the wall to my right dripping down
like cheap paint and stopping short before hitting the floor and
pooling at the seam where the wall meets the floor, but more like it
rounded up the surrounding air molecules then slowly traversed a
surface of sea urchins, their spiny round bodies ready to puncture
my lie as if a balloon, they don't because here I stand in front of you
in broad daylight admitting that it was a lie and it is in fact not the
lie itself that troubles because actually it was so tiny and so white,
but I am bothered by your alacrity in pointing it out, and this can
only lead to one thing which is that I am the heavy and someone
will break and you are the cause, beautiful long cause of this age-
old situation grinning at me through crooked teeth molded out of
someone else's mistake I admit though I hate it just the same there
is nothing for me to offer in this. Nothing for me to offer in this.

STAR CLUSTERS LIKE THE CLATTER

In the mouth of Girl H, gently being passed to the mouth of Girl I, who then turns to the pear skin lady just now removing her hat. The star clusters fall out of the mouth of the pear skin lady and into the hat, which is then placed in the middle of the room. No one is obligated to say anything, but the clatter of girls falls silent around the hat.

BLOW UP AND ACCELERATE

You are ringing and don't line up. I advance, you acknowledge—
enlarge—edge of this. I throat, you knee, I return to the gunboat
and you had stolen it. Too many girls in a frame. Information portal,
baseball bat. Box to box, stand. A clutch of girls too many, all over
the television. Or newspaper. A dart and a back and forth, claim to a
conscience. Here is my hand. Expended cabbage, conditional tender
to you.

SINK OR SWIM

水位上 升时, 汽车熄火, 只有 Girl F, Girl H,
和 Girl I 能够帮忙.

人海中, Girl A 常常在无名的路上讨饭. 突然 Girl C 会救她.
一阵风吹来.

最后路灯婚姻的光

　　　　搞乱——擦汗

　　假装（换）丈夫.

GIRL C CAUGHT WORKING IN THE SUN

Sometimes when you show up for work and the tops of the trains have blown off, and not only that but they have changed the train routes on you so not only are you no longer covered by that thing called ceiling, you are also no longer covered by that thing called underground tunnel, your workplace is no longer the subway but the national, aboveground train system, you are finding that you need to talk louder to be heard above the din of the world, you wish they had told you in advance so you could have worn sunscreen or brought a hat, the brim of the cap that is part of your uniform gives only the tiniest amount of shade that covers only your forehead and eyebrows, your greasy nose is shining in the sun, you are feeling a gush of air filling your lungs as if you were tree or animal, your hair blows back, the passengers blink, and the air resistance of the train has been so altered by the situation that you are not as precise in hitting your stops as you always are, any other day but today.

29 YEARS OF GIRLS

Living in the same body. I breathe in, they sway. I breathe out, they hang on. Organs, tissue, jungle. They link up so as to not fall apart: a stray girl lost in a body can wreak havoc on the system. For 29 years they have been linked and ready, pocketing anticipation whenever it came down the pipes, holding space inside the cheeks for just in case, primped, powdered, combed, polished, 29 years of growing only imperceptibly, 29 years of contingency plans, all the girls, some more ready than others but some ready enough for the whole lot of them, holding it as it balloons mushrooms heirlooms pretty circles above their heads their shining tresses, loving it the thought of it as it sends vibrations of anticipatory rain, leaving it, all the parts the detritus the bags in the rain, all the girls all 29 years of girls all piling up crowding together near the opening, wondering if finally it is time, wondering if finally it is here, wondering if finally there will be a new peace, a different peace, an unforeseen peace, peace of the word, waiting there on the other side, will it open will it spread what will it smell like on the other side of these 29 years of girls, 29 girl years on one side of the body, and then finally there is a there to go to to look at to see through to move into and through, all the way to that shining other side of it all.

A BOIL OF GLASS OR GIRL G
WHO IS FADING AWAY

Not by will, work, warp, not intention, nor outervention, not because
boiling glass more fashionable or sustainable or containable, not
because it isn't all that which beauties, or because it is, not because it
doesn't work, they don't work, not because it can't be fixed, they can't
be fixed, not because it is evil, mean, or ruthless, what are they, they
are crucial, sheen, upheaval, not because it is getting older and no
longer as beautiful as the youngest boil of glass, not because the
youngest boil of glass inevitably turns into a boil of glass much like
Girl G, not because there isn't money enough to sponsor the indefinite
youth of a boil of glass, not because there is not reason enough or
justification or rationalization enough or amicable feelings enough for
the boil of glass that is Girl G, as well as the glass of boil that is had by
Girl G, not because glass breaks and boils over, they take and change
over, not because of goodness or attempts toward fullness, not because
of or in spite of the glassy look behind the glass of Girl G who has
never truly felt it, never broke, never thorn, never hurt so fully as to
see what it's like to boil over, and out, spill, away, simply because it is
time for glass and boils to come to acknowledge their relation to Girl G
and how tenuous in light, and its fade.

GIRL J COVERED INSIDE
AND OUT IN ANTIMONY

Where the trouble begins is where the outside approaches the inside.
A helpful outsider tries to demarcate such distinctions, but gets
balled up and unceremoniously rolled away like wandering soot.
One is advised not to attempt intervention, especially not if such
an attempt stems from what are assumed to be good intentions.
Say it again and think twice. Girl J is not a child and does not need
strangers to look after her. Girl J has already taken care of her
outside. Girl J with antimonials. What happens next. Ingestion has
its limitations. Does she want to talk this out with someone. No.
Then what. Search for an agent. Said agent shall act as vehicle,
conduit, trailblazer, firehose. Said agent shall travel the far reaches of
the insides of Girl J, depositing antimony in an even coat. Said agent
shall not be paid, compensated, or thanked. Why thank someone for
spreading a toxic substance all over the insides of your body.

THERE ARE MULTIPLE GIRLS AND WAYS OF APPRECIATING OLIVIER MESSIAEN

Girl F's the getting, and tiredness is the reference, and the other is girled by their initials. There's the decisive finding, that is, the name-outer, the girl-eacher, the come-what-may, but there are also some extremely marching shes, which makes Girl J say very well why there was so much Hi, name, fuck, of you: at asking-for, it is yours. It is Girl F, swallowing. There's no hardness, no embarrassment, no whiling, just this listening . . . so, intentions were a little Girl J by whose whispers, because, amid all this bare audibility, justly, a case would want you.

THE EXTENT OF GIRLSKIN AS SHE ACCRUES AN INTEREST IN SAFETY

Spreads wider with each new encounter, so as to enfold them so as to prevent breakage so as to extirpate so as to attenuate so as to better calculate the quotients of her cheap store-bought love emergent across her body.

I find many things within the folds of her thick-again thin-again skin: half-eaten sandwich, directions to Joyful Gardens, bright red tote bag, nuts in their shells, coins. Clearly it has not been cleaned in years, but the nuts are still edible in a pinch.

This is a skin with its own intentions. This is a skin that knows when to stretch and when to hold. I gently poke my finger in, partly to test if anyone is observing through the security monitors. I fear that they can distinguish between my testing them and my pretending to look for a lost sandwich. I get the sense that they know, just the slightest split second before even I know.

Inside are some people. Fortunately, they are seated. Someone has created nice folds of skin to cushion the bony bottoms of the old folks—they must be the special ones. They look tired, though they should be protected by their status. I wonder just how much protection this skin can provide after all.

IN A PLASTIC BAG OF JELL-O
WITH NINE OTHER GIRLS

Once the rods in my eyes adjust to the gradations of green, I regret it. Things were easier when I couldn't see. Those choices are no longer available.

I inhale Jell-O, trusting I will get better at this, assuming the other nine girls have been here longer and they, too, struggled at first. I interrupt the writhing movements of Girl J, who looks like she is trying to appear to be having a good time. I ask, to no one in particular, if this Jell-O is safe to eat. No one answers.

The Jell-O is more muscular than I recall. Have my own muscles atrophied so much as to create this perception, or is it the fault of this minimal-gravity state of being suspended in Jell-O, or were they having a drought. No one answers. Did I ever manage to ask.

I see a sequence of cubes that might function as a staircase leading me up and out of this place. But it's not that I wanted to leave. If only I could find Girl D, we could sell this thing, all of us contained, as a work of art and make a Jell-O-ton of money. Or if I could find

Girl H and get a hold of a camera and document ourselves releasing emotions into gelatinous sugar, then smuggle the footage out of the bag, the rescue crew would know what to bring when they decide to come for us. I take a deep Jell-O breath and start to shout, *Has anybody seen* ... but then I remember that I am hoping to avoid Girl E, who is likely to blame this whole situation on me.

Although the exact hue cannot be ascertained until they pull us one by one out of the green Jell-O, I do suspect that my skin is turning green. Some girls are darker, some lighter. Their faces, their feet, all of their skin is changing color and I vaguely hope that I might come out of this a little sweeter. Meal preparation or science project, I bet we are not even going to make the evening news.

GIRL D HAS A JOB AND A STORE

Welcome to the store of departments. This is Girl D, and she will show you how to watch your step all the way to the realities section. Drop your hips an inch. Take a walk in the woods. The air may part limply to allow you to march forward. Do not fall for it. Do not fall in with your clothes on. The limp is not in your imagination. If you walk too slowly, the air will wrap itself around you in a show of faux chivalry which you might not think to fend off immediately, but you should imagine it as a material whose viscosity increases with time. Do fixate on the particularity of the beauty that arises midgait, bursting hot and naked through the cracks of amplified notes decaying off the jazz singer's broadcasts. That beauty is easy to miss. Your recognition of that fact will propel you forward, vividly, humbly. I see your face. I see your hand. I see you open to keep it to loosen its graceful sweep.

ガールスープ

いろいろ決めるのが面倒になって、どこで食べたいって聞かれたら、どこで
もいいって返事する、もうこうなったらなんだって食べられるって言う。す
ると目の前に現れたのはガールスープ、あー、でも、やっぱりそれだけは無
理。同じテーブルに座った人たちは、さっさとボウルの中の女の子たちをめ
がけて食べはじめる。ほっておくとサイボーグやロボットに変身して、そう
なったら噛むのが大変ってことを知っているから。中にはまだ生きている女
の子たちもいて、スープから脱出したいのかなって思うけど、よく見ると床
だって女の子たちでいっぱい、洋服にスープをべったりつけて（まさか裸だ
と思ってなかったよね？）、だからそれはやめておく。もうどうしようもな
いっていうその瞬間、何を思ったか深く息を吸って飛び込む、そう、ガール
スープの中にぽちゃんと、IDなんていらないし、服のサイズとか性別とか
人種とか誰に投票するのかなんて誰にも聞かれない、そしてボウルの中で女
の子たちを集めて大きな円陣を組む。こうしてふたつの主要な問題が解決さ
れた。大きな塊となったわたしたちは絶対に食べられないし、そしてもう食
べる人だっていなくなった。

GIRL IN HER DREAMINGS
AND GIRL IN HER HAIR

The mistake is in both belief and memory. At that Girl H lies down flat she is like that. On the bed, she sinks in. In the street, she gets run over. Over a body—body of water—her hair spreads, largest and smallest as a convergent point burned by the unbearable light. Her dreamings do not fracture, they leach slowly into the water, the street, the sheets. Even more slowly, they are welcomed or rejected based on their color. When she catches on to what is happening, she takes to hiding her dreamings in her hair. Her hair goes long, longer, all the better to hide more and more believings.

GIRL A AND THE MONEY

Ferris Wheel of Fortune. How many revolutions are enough. Girl A
ponies up for another ride. I'm at the top. I'm not at the top. She
takes her stuffed rabbits and goes in again. She takes the outline of
her future baby and goes in again. She takes her empty wallet and
goes in again. Again and again she enters, again and again at the
zenith of the ride she lifts her hands to the ceiling.

The cage fills with objects and animals. Tacos leak out the sides.
There are mouth guards, kneepads, fertility swabs. Frogs.

Having been accomplice to her own burial in the moving cage, Girl A
is nearly invisible; her hands can barely find the edges. Eventually
she makes out a figure on the ground. Every time she approaches
the ground she sees this figure a little more clearly: the one with the
money.

At this point Girl A has been on the ride so long that the center of
the universe has shifted. If she could remove all the objects and
animals from her cage, she could possibly extend her reach, make a
grab for it. I hold on to one taco. Some objects have appeared out of

nowhere. Like the broom that fell out of the sky, making a hole in the top of the cage. Girl A sees trains shooting out to the horizon. I see trains shooting out to the horizon. Nevermind the rising and falling of the horizon. Nevermind the trains that fall off the edge of empty space.

When the Ferris Wheel of Fortune falls over, those stuffed bunnies are going to save her, and me, and all of us, just you watch. And only by the grace of the fact that she never took the money, we're going to see it, mark my words, see an unharmed Girl A pop out of that cage and make a run for it, far beyond the confines of the event itself.

BRIGHT SUN IN THE HEAD OF THE GIRLS

But that is not all. Bright
den stones, bright precious
finally gets to sleep with Girl
mered into gossamer threads
Girl H reach through to the
the marrow of Girl F. The lines
and encourage mutual spar-
ary to that of Girl F and Girl
They are not up in the head,
protect themselves from being
dried cow shit, bright hid-
clay whistles. When Girl F
H, the bright wounds ham-
wrapped around the heart of
bright lines leaving tracks on
and threads fall into each other
kling until their love, second-
H, heats up into a tiny little sun.
as advertised, but that is how they
discovered and potentially harmed.

GIRL P―白く溶ける日

ここで、少女Pは生まれなかった。ここは大陸である。少女Pは大陸の端の半島で生まれて大陸で育った。ここは大陸のどことも違う場所だった。１９世紀の終わり、大陸の激変する歩みとともに名を知らしめ、２０世紀文化を象徴するモダン・シティだった。ここでは、大陸の人間より、移り住んだ人間の方が目立っていた。路地にうごめく人間より、アカシアの並木道をはさんでレンガ造りの家を構える人間の方が目立っていた。少女Pはアカシアの並木道を歩いた。レンガ造りの家にはロシアのことばが灯った。ドイツのことばが灯った。レンガ造りの家々のあいだには大陸のことばが行き交った。少女Pがレンガ造りの家に帰ると、両親のことばに包まれた。いや、つかまれた。扉を閉めると、もう大陸のことばは聞こえてこない。暖炉の火に手をあてて、冷たい両頬にあてる。暖炉の薪がときおり動く。透明な火柱に近い色だ。どこまで火の温もりは届くのだろう。ぼんやりする少女Pの両頬はもう火照っている。両親のことばが耳にころがってくる。食事の時間だ。

顔をくしゃくしゃにして笑う、
それは、ひまわり
それは、背丈がある
それは、ゆっくりと
それは、白く溶ける日のこと

ここで、少女Pは成長とともに、大陸のことばも身につけた。家事をしにく
る大陸の小姐（シャオジェ）と仲良く冗談まで言えるほどだ。両親は女の子
たちの会話に冷たい視線を投げて肩をすくめる。両親は大陸のことばをある
程度知っている。生き抜くために。ここで、生き抜くために。ここで、とき
には本当の出自を隠して生きていくために。まっぴらごめんだ、まっぴらご
めんだ、まっぴらごめんだ。父は三回唱える。わたしのせいじゃない、母は
うなりながら唱える。気が遠くなる。

置き去りにされたことばをひとつひとつ拾い上げて
頬ずりしてみよう
古い麻の
においがするから

ある日のこと、
小姐がちいさな虎の子をもってきた。ちいさな手のひらにのる、布の虎の子
人形。煮しめたような色。麻の古着をほどいて作ってみたという。むかし、
むかし、おばあちゃんが言いました。わたしたちの虎の子はどこにいったの
だろう、わたしたちの虎の子はいなくなりました、わたしたちの虎の子はお
ばあちゃんをさがしています、わたしたちの虎の子はおまえをけっして忘れ
やしない。

ここで、

ひまわりが　おちる

ひまわりが　あたまが おちる

ひまわりが　まっさかさまに おちる

ひまわりが　きいろい ちが ちらばる

ひまわりが　きいろい ちが つちに にじむ

にほんとうを　ふりかざして　おじちゃんは だまって　ひまわりを　きりお
とした

ひまわりは　わたしより　せが　たかい

ひまわりは　おねえちゃんと　せが　ならぶ

ひまわりは　きりおとされ　たおれながら　さけぶ

ほんとうは　おねえちゃんが　さけぶ

おじちゃん　おじちゃん　おじちゃん

にほんとうを　ふりかざして　おじちゃんは　だまって　つったっている

おじちゃんは　なぜ　ないているのか

おじちゃんは　せんそうが　おわったことを　しったから

おじちゃんは　しんじてきたこと　すべてを　ひていされたから

おじちゃんは　むなしくて にほんとうを ふりかざしたのか

おじちゃんは　ひまわりを　ころした
ほんとうは　おねえちゃんを　ころした
ほんとうは　わたしのことも　ころした
あかい　すなが　まいあがり
あったことを　なかったことにした

あの　なつのひから
わたしたちは
なかった
ひとたち

GIRL B AND GIRL J HAVE PARALLEL MEALS

With unparallel means. When Girl B reaches across the table to the hand of a lover, Girl J gives a swift kick under the table to her asshole editor and that is a parallel meal. When Girl B eats to about thirty percent capacity, Girl J is busy barfing up the irreconcilable differences between a taste for pornography and tastefulness in pornography, and that, too, is a parallel. Girl B chews, Girl J chases. Girl B spits, Girl J interrogates, Girl B gargles, Girl J swallows. Girl B on the brink of overcooking that idea out of the realm of tenability. Girl J bonking head against the inherited pressures of her profession.

When the pink kappa shows up unannounced, Girl B and Girl J both lunge a desperate hand towards her, forgetting that the arms of a kappa are connected and removable, forgetting what all we learned from Red Rover Red Rover, Ring Around the Rosie, Ho Yay, *The Caucasian Chalk Circle*, Hands Across America, and the 38th parallel.

LAID OUT ALONG THE ROAD
LIKE ATTENUANT PARTS

Is the residue we bandolier warned you about. Watch out for
assurgent matters—like when the sunscrabble hits the road hard
and you find yourself undappled, unready to escape being hit
by the sharpness of your own refractions. Venesection. Hold your
sanguijuelas. Each girl is a vehicle, house, or anti-occupant. Leech into
louse into decision fatigues. When the sunlight is not hitting the road,
it is possible to visit or re-imagine what used to be the girl, the ruse,
or the fullness of enclosure. By the time someone kindly asks you to
go invisible, you may have already merged with the residue. Whether
you find this appropriate or not, desirable or not, incommensurable
or not, don't you say it, spark say you—we didn't warn you.

GIRL A'S PEANUTS AND
GIRL D'S MOUTHFUL

Girl A on the train with peanuts. The expectant fullness of Girl D's
mouth. Growing distance of the floor. A few bystanders are scraped
by peanut shell, but believing themselves innocent, are willing to let
peanut scars be peanut scars. How good of them. Girl A soon bereft
of all peanuts. Girl D, too, close to the brink. And when it happens,
it will not only rain peanuts, but also nails, bones, hair clippings,
gavels, hammers, and broken-tongue talkers will all come shooting
out of her mouth and fall down on everyone, on all of us, inside and
outside and throughout the train and the rain and the girls and
across the dead oceans, training up for the hard rain, for the new
weather, for the new weather.

少女営巣弓

少女唇震山々

一人不安喪失繊細事実

一人滑降直下

一人眼球押捺指紋

以下参照事実

一少女賜物

一少女城市

一少女城市訪問城市

一少女悲哀

一少女井戸

帽子粉飾鳩翼≠少女

既報告済

少女遊歩欧州城市≠少女

蝙蝠少女＝遊歩欧州城市少女

歩歩歩歩女女女女眼眼眼眼眼

停止虹弓下

私常時女子混合思考

私貴女脂肪熱震

私弓形貴方触手

火傷

私限界→女性視線大理石像

私凝視貴女

貴女捜索出口

私達外界

私達脱出

GIRL F IN A SEA OF WALDAS

In a dance performance choreographed by a sensitive oyster. From the pearl, one set of instructions is issued to Girl F, another set goes to the Waldas. Girl F is surrounded by Waldas; one might describe it as "Wall-to-Wall Waldas," except there are no walls. Girl F is instructed to find the Waldo in this sea of Waldas, an assignment she is not particularly keen to accept. And if she should find him, then what? What will she do—dance with him? Lick his stripes off? Bash the white smugness out of him with his own cane?

The Waldas have formed beautiful rows in the audience seating. They each have a baby oyster in their lap. They sigh their collective sighs, getting louder and louder until the whacking sound is drowned out, until the Waldo fades to dust, and they are each dancing with Girl F, spinning and spinning in a sea of raging pink pearls.

GIRLS RESPOND QUICKLY
TO A CALL FROM UP HIGH

A long silk skirt billows out in all directions—
              this wind rose, a garden of cardinal points
singing against convention—i.e., southeast, northwest,
                        southwest, northeast
      not the stars of north, south, east, and west
in a typical fashion. They unravel their long hair, sending
              each strand into a live stream of clouds.

Fragrance widens under a hemline—as if nothing is
      out of the ordinary
except the girl up above is on fire   dancing or drowning
the girls in sum   rising into and upward while burning
perfume, a weight on the weave of the silken fabric
        of their own clothing.

Flames sizzle over the plaza   aromatic trees, the birds, the clouds
smoking while levitating
the invisible elevator of a girl on fire in the midst
      of a disordered alphabet: I, J, G, D, B
I repeat: B, D, G, J, I. Yes, now I see—

Upward in a long, thin line

all the way up   glory

      there's a girl on fire   her soul intact

this is the way

       things are going to be.

WORLD MADE UP OF PIECES
OF GIRLS B, D, E, AND G

Girl G volunteers to be ◎, urg●g Girl B to go for anti-◎, whereas
Girl D can be negative space and then maybe Girl E will spr●kle
herself like ●visible fairy dust all over the top of the cake, which
is the k●d of th●g that happens when girls like Girl E fail to get
properly educated about the com●gs and go●gs of ◎ and anti-◎.
Girl D sits back and crosses her arms and shakes her head ● disda●
at the idea first of fairy dust and second of relegat●g the female
body to some condition of stuff that is needlessly dim●ished,
spark●g the righteous anger of Girl G who has also now realized that
● this particular circumstance they are not be●g asked to be wholly
◎ or even full of ◎, but to be t●y zillions of pieces of ◎, which is not
at all what they signed up for, and as the situation starts to
crystallize ●to clearer ●sight ● the m●d of Girl G, she beg●s a
secret campaign to collect, amass, and connect all the little pieces of
Girl B, Girl D, Girl E, and herself and then work up a movement to
compress themselves until they have done a bang-up job of it, and
now you can f●d them there on the side of the road, right there, that
beautiful unpolished hunk of exposed aggregate.

GIRL F WALKS INTO A BAR

Girl F pushes open an unmarked door, entering a bar full of Asian men in America. As she moves slowly through space, contemplating where to sit, she feels a gentle pat on her back.

When she has made her decision and is seated, she spikes both their drinks with ancient herbal roots to signal she is ready to hitchameromperodeo, and everyone else, of all genders and races, starts vigorously shaking their head.

FOUR GIRLS POOL THEIR BREASTS TOGETHER

For a total of eight. To avoid awkwardness, stares, and uselessness, they are quick to round up some babies. The babies know how to get a good latch, but the girls who are new at this have trouble getting their elbows out of the way. They worry about explaining their bruised faces at work the next day—group breastfeeding accident? Truth is in a stranger. Girl D's mother comes along and drapes a soft gauzy blanket over the whole pile of girls and babies, but the motive is not modesty—the heads of the babies cover up enough of the breasts for enough of the time. Rather, the intention of the mother is to shield them all from the impending storm, while still allowing for air circulation. That kind of mother-gauze.

The breastfeeding babies, while nursing, breathe through their nostrils. Without this ability, said baby would be forced to choose—breathe or nurse—the two cannot be done concurrently. Over the decades, the collective, heavy, and steady nose-breathing of the babies slowly wears down the gauzy blanket.

One baby mindlessly fingers a hole in the gauze while continuing to suckle milk from Girl I.

One baby is face-fucking the breast of a highly influential art curator, but has neither the language nor the awareness so as to make it count.

One baby is distracted by the sound of another baby fondling the gauze, and breaks away from the spell of the breast, catches a glimpse of the moon shimmering through a hole in the gauze.

One baby is crushed by the weight of another baby. This in itself is not really the problem, it is just that under the pressure of the weight of the other baby, she can feel her own center of gravity sliding away, threatening to elongate or separate her body away from her head, her mouth, her lips clamped around the tired breast of Girl H. Her body stretches out. The nipple of Girl H stretches out. Something has to give, and it will, but sometimes this takes years, maybe nine or ten or more.

MAP

There is a girl I look for on the map of unspoken indignities but I can't find her, because she is all over it, dismembered into tiny little millions of fragments and scattered all over the place. Usually this is referred to as a *barabara jiken*, a dismembered-into-tiny-millions-of-fragments incident. Although *bara* is homonymous with *rose*, this is not a rose-rose incident. Also please stop correcting me on how to pronounce my name.

SOFT WHITE FEEL FLOWER RUN

Girl J and Girl A touch fingertip to fingertip. The eye on each fingertip blinking and pressing and blinking.

Girl I opens her mouth and flowers rush in. Mouth closes. Those that did not make it fade away. As Girl I chews, the fragrance entices some creatures to approach, some to run away.

Girl F and her nose amble through town. They caress a wall that they mistake for a sofa, sit on a hood that they mistake for a flowerbed. When suddenly the engine starts and the vehicle accelerates, they cling to each other, hoping not to be flung into the chain-link fence that they would like to mistake for open arms.

Girl D loses her vision in the shuffle. She kisses the trunk and buys the whole animal. When it arrives at work the next day, it escapes the notice of all who are perpetually seated.

Girl C is stuck on a train that glides past the blinking eyes of Girl A and Girl J, the chewing mouth of Girl I, the bouncing butt of Girl F and her nose, the misguided vision of Girl D. Girl C does not know what she sees. Girl C forgets to run.

GIRL B UNDER THE ARCH

May appear to be speaking casually to me as we chat about our weekend plans, oh you're going to the city to see the show where the deaf Korean woman threads her arms through the pits of a big white man and uses ASL to sign intricate descriptions of cats and dogs, like "Cat that has been so traumatized by hot dogs that the sight of a child eating a hot dog sends her skittering away, that cat" or "Dog that looks miserable but is not actually unhappy at all, is wet not because it was raining but because the neighbors had their sprinklers on and it was impossible to resist, that dog." And, oh you're going to the wedding of your friend who is a pure mathematician and also an acrobat who can do frontflips but not backflips, whose mother claims to not have tossed her around in frontflips when she was a baby, she denies it but how else could it be so innately easy and effortless? And thus the conversation charms and hums, meanwhile I do notice that the hand of Girl B is sticking out ever so slightly, at a perfect angle so as to catch any diamonds that fall down from the arch, the arch under which we chat, from the looks of it we are so very innocent, and it's one thing if she catches one or two, but the whole reason I am here is to keep close watch, should she ever try to slip one into her mouth, my muscles may seem relaxed but they are all coiled up ready to pounce, should it be necessary, I'm all over it.

BRIGHT SUN IN THE HEAD OF THE GIRLS

これは、さっきあった詩、 Bright Sun In The Head Of The Girls というや
つのとっても適当ないい加減な翻訳です。訴訟をおこしてごらん。あはは。

The preceding lines explain the fact that this, what you are reading,
or hearing, or witnessing, is a totally irresponsible and mediocre
translation of the poem from earlier, called "Bright Sun In The Head
Of The Girls." And then at the end of the line I said "sue me" in
Japanese, which caused a giggle. It is only after the mediocre translator
gives up on translating that anything of value ever happens.

まあとにかくかくかくしかしそれだけではなく。あっかるーい。からっから
に乾燥した牛の糞。 That was the bright dried cow shit, 牛の糞、right.
And then the bright hidden stones is the あっかるーい。かくーしきった
きれーいな石ころころころ、心の中には貴重な粘土の笛、口笛（がんばって
吹いてごらん！）(That was the bright precious clay whistles—did you
blow it or did you blow it.)

でもやはり翻訳はここまでとします。10:54糞、もう夜遅いしあなたの野暮っ
たさに疲れたし実は今日結構ツラかったし When Girl F finally gets
to sleep with Girl H, the bright wounds hammered into gossamer

threads wrapped around the heart of Girl H reach through to the bright lines leaving tracks on the marrow of Girl F.

I am actually just reading the original lines in English now, the mediocre translator having given up already, only halfway into the poem. Worse, they are dropping their shit, that's the word 糞、 which is also homonymous with the counter for minutes, so they stuck that in there after the 10:54, they said 10時54糞、 a stupid pun that indicates how they feel about being asked to play the role of the shitty translator at this late hour. See how easy it is to shit in a poem of mediocre translation.

ここで線と糸が転がりかけ落ち会いながらお互いにキラキラと輝きだして
そもそもその愛情そのものが熱をためてためて小さな可愛い太陽になって、
その太陽は鳥の巣のような頭の家にある筈なのが実際問題そんなことをす
ると危険で見つかってしまうので

The lines and 英語の文章の threads fall into each other and encourage mutual sparkling until their love, 中に、 heats up into a tiny little sun. They are not up in the head, as advertised, but that is how they protect themselves 隠れてみよう from being discovered and potentially harmed.

LAID OUT ALONG THE ROAD
LIKE ATTENUANT PARTS

減衰 (ゲンスイ) (degree of attenuation) (rank in the Imperial
　　Japanese Army) (raw water) (reduction in water level)

部品 (ぶひん) (parts)

道幅 (みちはば) (road width)

広例 (コウレイ) (extensive examples) (interaction between the
　　living and the dead) (amicable example) (large and wonderful)
　　(routine occurrence) (ghosts of royalty) (tall ridge) (elderly)

残余 (ざんよ) (residue)

言言 (いったいったよ) (word)

太陽 (タイヨウ) (sun) (state of being)

道当 (ドウトウ) (many) (sameness)

反射光 (はんしゃこう) (reflected light)

逃切 (とうせつ) (escape)

注意 (ちゅうい) (precautions)

各女子 (かくじょし) (every girl)

乗物 (のりもの) (vehicle)

家 (いえ) (home)

居住者 (きょじゅうしゃ) (resident)

太陽 (たいよう) (sun)

道当 (どうとう) (many)

場合 (ばあい)

過去 (かこ)

女子 (じょし)

家 (いえ)

囲込 (かこいこみ) (shell)

膨 (ふくよか) (swell)

再想像 (さいそうぞう) (reimagining)

再現 (さいげん) (see you later)

可能 (かのう) (possible)

丁寧 (ていねい) (polite)

追出 (おいだし) (exile)

時点 (じてん) (time)

残余 (ざんよ) (residue)

合併 (がっぺい) (merge)

適切 (てきせつ) (appropriate)

好 (このましい) (good, this is good)

可能 (かのう) (possible)

誰言 (すいげん) (whose words)

言不言 (？) (latent language)

THE DEAD GIRL YOU ARE DRAGGING
OFF THE BACK OF YOUR BOAT

Stop asking me if it is Girl A or B or C or D. It is none of your business. Drive the boat. There are more girls about to rain. Are you a dodger or a catcher. Row the boat to the right or to the left. Look. Do you see that parachute opening. Can you do the math. Calculate your rowing speed and her falling speed. Can you catch her. Will she break the boat. Will you get bounced out. Will you open your mouth. Will you feed her. Will you still be there.

The girl coming down with the weather is the offspring of Girl A or B or C or D, and is old enough to drive her own boat. She spreads her arms and legs wide to slow her descent, though all of us know that her descent will not be slowed by some trivial amount of air resistance.

Space invaders arrive and are quickly whisked away.

Children of uncertain ancestry arrive with their toy AK-47s and are also whisked away.

A tribe of singers arrives and calls to the girl coming down with the weather. The weather comes down with her in response. The direction of impact is unclear.

Scottish bagpipes are drowned out by Korean girl rappers. In the end it is they, the Korean girl rappers, who command control of the boat. The girls are caught, loved, then beautiful. The rain slides off their backs and turns to krill. The shrimp do a little dance. Small children do a little dance. Snatching and throwing and grilling and eating, dancing and singing, dancing and singing.

TEN GIRLS IN A BAG OF POTATO CHIPS

Fight over who gets which chip, as if there were no more than ten chips in the bag. There are more than ten chips in the bag.

Girl A assumes that the bigger, the rounder, the better. Girl G believes that the beautiful ones should choose first. Girl C makes a bid for lung capacity. Girl J sees that the sharp edges of the less round, more imperfect chip might come in handy one day. She remains quiet. Girl I says no.

Only Girl H takes note of the fact that the crispness of the chips is proof positive that the container, I mean the bag, that they reside in, is airtight. Only Girl H has a feeling for her true position within the global economy and food supply chain and how it affects the likely outcome of their collective fate. She has trouble deciding whether to speak, slap, or remain silent.

OCHIKUBO STEW

Excessive exhaustion over last night's dream featuring those pretty
round masticators and their ninety-degree turns. It emerges with
exactitude from this faux moment of reconciliation, which is why
today is the day I've really had enough of this decision-making
feculence and when they ask me where, when, what, or whether,
I say fuck you, you can eat my apron strings for all I care.

Cha, cha, cha, cha, next thing I know I am seated at an inability
table, face-to-face with Ochikubo stew. Others at the table speed the
consumption of specifically the Ochikubos, due to their awareness
of masticability issues (as noted in the "still alive" model or more
recent "girl liberation" models) or feasibility; if we wait too long we
will have to search for them among the mice and horses scampering
boldly off the table.

Cha, cha, cha, cha, some of the Ochikubos wriggle around. I squint.
They are all over the floor, pumpkin bits clinging to their dresses. A
quiet chant against forced female nudity is emitted from the depths
of the bowl. Time is measured by the duration required for an
Ochikubo to wear down a mountain by giving it a swipe with her
dirty sleeve once every one hundred years.

Cha, cha, cha, cha, under the threat of exhausting all options, an inversion washes over the room. I peek far inside my own respirate oscillation and identify the solution, assuming I am allowed entry. No one here is kabocha, cha, cha-ing their Seven Theses on Extrication. While the Ochikubo Stew still harbors tumult, the fact remains that we have temporarily resolved this acute predicament, less a problem now with the removal of both the principle masticator and the wrongly-configured economies of scale. Carefully we cha-cha our way out of the stew and into the getaway buggy made of dandelion tufts.

WHAT A CRAZY COUNTRY

Girls A through J in a new land. As good and conscientious visitors, they dutifully abide by the laws of the new land. It would only be polite.

And that is why when Girl A vomits, Girl B extends her cupped hands to catch it: in this land, it is not permissible for vomit to touch the ground. Girl B then passes the vomit into Girl C's cupped hands, who passes it to Girl D's cupped hands. And so on. The hands of the girls who have already passed it forward are covered in a layer of vomit. They wait patiently for it to dry. They are not permitted to wash their hands.

Round and round the vomit goes, until there is not enough left to pass on. When the passing of the vomit is complete, the girls move to a sunnier location so as to speed up the drying of the vomit layers on their hands. And then, finally, move on with their lives.

Girl E is still processing what has happened to them in this new land, when a local informant whispers something in her ear. What she hears makes Girl E almost vomit—she tastes it at the back of her throat—but she just barely manages to swallow it back down.

MOUNTAIN GIRLS

People ask where I'm from and I've no choice but to say that I'm
from the mountains, and then depending on the number of twitches
I count on their face, I lie and say I'm from this mountain or that
mountain, in this or that state. The facial expression that leads
me to fess up and say I am from Awa're-zan, the mountain where
desperately starving young men would carry their old grandmas on
their backs and leave them deep in the woods to wither and die,
except that these old grandmas developed their own community of
mountain hags and managed to live a grand old life, burrowing into
the mountainside only when they were truly done with life and
not when some ungrateful unresourceful son had decided to get
rid of them, and yeah I'm one of those girls that is actually a reborn
mountain hag—well that facial expression is quite wonderful and
amazing and I have yet to come up with a name for it—what about
you, where are you from?

GIRL P—WHOSE STORY NEVER ENDS

Girl P was not born here. This is a continent. Girl P was born and lived on a peninsula on the continent's edge. This place somehow different from the continent. It made its name alongside the changes and upheavals on the continent at the end of the nineteenth century—a "modern city" symbolizing twentieth-century culture. Here, those who had migrated were more conspicuous than those from the continent. Girl P walks the acacia-lined streets. Russian words visibly lit upon the brick houses. German words, too. The language of the continent flickering between the brick houses. Upon returning to her own brick house, the language of her parents envelops Girl P. No, entraps. She closes the door against the language of the continent. She moves her hands from the warm fireplace to her cold cheeks. Sometimes, the firewood shifts. The color of a transparent column of fire. How far up does the warmth extend. Girl P's mind wanders and her cheeks are flushed. Her parents' voices tumble into her ears. It is time for dinner.

*Here   sunflowers   fall   sunflowers   fall   on my head   sunflowers
fall   upside down   sunflowers   their   yellow blood   scatters
sunflowers   their   yellow blood   stains the earth*

The   silent   man   with the Japanese sword   fells   sunflowers

*Sunflowers   are taller   than me   sunflowers   are as tall as   my sister
sunflowers   are fallen   they scream   as they fall   in reality   it is my
sister   who screams   hey you   you   you*

The   silent   man   with the Japanese sword   silently   stands

*That man   why does he cry   that man   who learned   the war had
ended   that man   who had to disavow   all that he believed   that man
wielding   the Japanese sword   in vain*

*That man   killed   the sunflowers   in reality   it is my sister   he killed
in reality   it is me too   that he killed   red dirt   rises   what happened
was said to have not happened   that   summer   day since   we   ceased
to exist*

As Girl P grew here, she learned the language of the continent. To the
point where she could exchange friendly jokes with the xiaojie from
the continent who came to help around the house. The parents
looked coldly upon the girls' conversations. The parents knew of the
language of the continent to some degree. To survive. To survive
here. Here, sometimes, to keep their identity hidden. I refuse.

GIRL D AND HER PHOSPHORUS EYES

Do not make eye contact with Girl D and her phosphorus eyes. Moreover, avoid receiving extended gazes from the phosphorus eyes of Girl D. They did not teach you about Girl D and her phosphorus eyes in school, not even on the day you were sick. There is no teachable moment. Just stay away. The only way you could possibly beat the system is if Girl D falls in love with you, but for Girl D to fall in love with you, you must risk the consequences of Girl D looking at you with her phosphorus eyes, and worse yet, making eye contact with Girl D and her phosphorus eyes, and this is exactly how most people die, and why no one has yet to have had Girl D fall in love with them. It is just like that.

GIRL F WAITS ON THE STREET CORNER OF LIMBER INTENTIONS

I acknowledge her as I crawl by, she acknowledges me as I roll myself into a ball of tin foil, tightly pack myself in, to weather the impending fight. The team of tin foil balls is usually disqualified pretty early, and that's just fine with me, I'm wussy that way. That said, there are a great many tin foil balls gathering behind Girl F here on this corner that is quickly becoming a platform, which makes me just a touch anxious. Last time we only used four, but this time I can't count what must be hundreds, thousands of tin foil balls, oh here come a few Girl Scouts with the foil from last night's roasted turkey dinner. Ball it up, little girls. Who roasts turkey on a regular non-holiday weeknight. That kind of troop leader. The kind of troop leader I need to keep Girl F away from.

To the naked eye, Girl F may look like an innocent girl on an innocent corner, but I have been made of tin foil for quite a long time now, and let me tell you. Soon the corner will be an isle. Then an island, then a mountain. Let's just hope I make it back safely and I will tell you everything, about every single forehead I have had the privilege of hitting and bouncing, hitting and bouncing, off of and off of and off of again.

29 YEARS OF GIRLS

Every seven years, a body changes all its cells,
        so we're physiologically different organisms

every seven years, although thanks to memory
        we're still ourselves. If I were twenty-nine again

I'd go to a place in the high desert, way out east
        at the foothills of the mountains where snow

springs are bottled and sold to those of us out
        west by the beaches. We can't drink all the water

in the bay, nor in the sea, although there's a lot
        of dihydrogen monoxide if we could use it. Once

I said dihydrogen monoxide to another woman
        who thought I was referring to poison. No,

H two O, I explained. It's the molecular
        formula for water. Not poison. Furrowing

her forehead, she frowned at me and said,
    I'm twenty-nine years old. I am not about

to attempt death by water. Rebirth, I said,
    you'll experience life by immersion, not

by drowning. I said, if I were twenty-nine
    again, I'd spend an extra year planning

for thirty so I could enjoy my latter years
    without trepidation, but rather, in peace.

GIRL NAMES

Girl F gets tired of referring to the other girls by their initials, and decides to find out the name of each girl, come what may. She marches up to Girl J and says, Hello, my name is Fuck You For Asking, what is yours? Girl F swallows hard on her embarrassment while she listens intently to Girl J, who whispers barely audibly: I'm Just In Case You Wanted To Hear More About My Vagina Than You Ever Imagined Possible. Girl F blinks twice towards the sweet innocent eyes of Girl J, then looks over at Girl H, who shakes her head.

THE SAWAKO NAKAYASU TOUR

When the tour group arrives at a certain part of the body of Sawako Nakayasu, a debate breaks out. Some girls claim that they have every right to visit every segment of the Sawako Nakayasu Tour, they sprang for the full tour, not the cheaper partial tour, mind you. Some girls claim that only girls with all biological girl parts have the right to visit all parts of the Sawako Nakayasu Tour. Some girls point to a document signed by Sawako Nakayasu granting all self-identifying girls access to all parts of the Sawako Nakayasu Tour. One girl suggests that they ask Sawako what they should do, but Sawako is in the middle of teaching class and part of the tour agreement was that Sawako is not to be disturbed at all, even while hosting four rounds of these tours every day, hence the document.

Business is booming, tours are booked solid for months in advance. The tour participants are in danger of blazing unwanted paths upon the body of Sawako Nakayasu. The inevitable end to each tour comes when one of the girls points a wet finger into the air and says hold up everybody, how can it be that we've all paid so much money for this, that money is being amassed (by whom?) because of our foolish demand for the Sawako Nakayasu Tour. And that is the moment, one of those moments when you can hear the sound of the dreams of a tour group getting shattered, and everyone scrambles to get their shoes back on so that they can tumble out and away from here, regrouping and setting out once again in search of a better way to put their money where their mouths are, never even pausing to wonder if one of those girls might have been a shill.

ALL THE GIRLS AND THEIR AUDIENCE MEMBER

Here lies Girl J. She has rolled up too soon, she will return later. You can shoot your delifrackenbunch towards her fury if you must.

Do you see the move in this crawl. Finally, your hand will burn: panicked, flipped, drowned, soaked. And unable to speak is Girl D's ablesmack, in stop-pause. Lift her hand.

You may observe their bamcockletights. Should circumstances hook, though, it is your obligation and belt to cut your strength immediately.

Their shut is feels, it is not a push.

Girl F, Girl H, and Girl I are here to float and tongue. Whatever you do, do not close your pitches with some open gathering of pantucketry and say to Girl H that she looks feverish from some emergency. She doesn't, let's just take that back right now.

81

ポテチの袋の中の10人の女の子

まるで袋の中には10枚のポテチしか入っていないかのように、どのポテチを誰が食べるかで言い争う。袋の中には10枚以上のポテチが入っている。

女の子Aは、当然、より大きくて丸いのが良いと思っている。女の子Gは、可愛い子たちが先に選ぶべきだと考えている。女の子Cは、肺活量で勝負をつけようとしている。女の子Jは、あまり丸くない「不完全な」ポテチのぎざぎざが、いつか役に立つ日が来るとみているが、黙ったままでいる。女の子Iは、選ぶのを断る。

女の子Hだけが、入れ物、つまり彼女たちが入っている袋が、密閉されている確たる証拠は、ポテチのパリパリ具合にあると気づいている。女の子Hだけが、グローバル経済と食品業界のサプライチェーンについての自分のはっきりした考えと、そうしたことが今後起こりうる自分たちの未来にどう影響するか感づいている。彼女は、話そうか、ひっぱたこうか、黙ったままでいようか、決めかねている。

GIRL FIGHT

Grandmother is parting her hair again. These days the ground absorbs not a single thing. Look.

Girl J is balling up Girl A's vomit into perfect little balls, rows and rows of vomit balls. The strong sunlight will dry and harden them in no time. The best, roundest, densest, hardest little vomit balls in the world. When the time comes, we will show those piss cube girls what we're made of. Don't ever forget what those girls' people have done to our girls' people. Make sure that our vomit balls are hard enough and smooth enough. (Remind me to tell you later about the jagged vomit balls.)

Are you ready. The wind is at our backs. Though if we beat the piss cube girls, next up are the diarrhea bomb girls. Grandmother is waving at us. She has finally found it—the scar on her head from back in the day, from her rock fights, it used to be so much simpler back then, people treated each other decently, it was much less complicated, they threw rocks at each other, and those very rocks, after the fighting, would just go back into the earth as if nothing had ever happened.

How times have changed. Just look at the ground when we are done fighting, just look.

HORNS, DELIVERY OF

Don't look directly at the horns of the girls. The aggregate time
you spend with your retina trained on any of their horns will, by
some estimates, be equivalent to the number of people who will get
plonked on the head by a raining speech-act, slurry, or unseasonable
declaration. Calculated in one act per microsecond.

The horns of Girl G, however, are relatively innocuous. She gets
them delivered weekly to her home. You can look, even stare, at
them with no direct consequence. Sometimes she covers them with a
homemade felt cozy, but that's just for effect and there is no physical
harm in having retinal contact with the horns of Girl G. This offer,
however, is not valid in the spiritual, ethical, micro- and macro-
emotional realms of your well-being and that of the world, so I would
still caution you against removing the felt cozy from the horns of
Girl G, even if she invites you. Especially if she invites you.

GURL E SEYLING SAMESONG OS UN ONGENE UN THIS BAECH WUD

This sackniss if Gurl E's silonce on this prociss if comong ti turms wiss this fuct if beong un who seys samesong os un ongene un this baech wud.

See foils ti cummunicote wiss precisiun this exuct dote see hoops ti miit Gurl K beong un who seys songs as un ongene un this baech wud.

Emaginong hurself ti be dispoisalleyed und ravelleyed bai oll hur murtal onomies thur Furrogamo hiils clackong umonously on hur draems, Gurl E saerches fur weys ti spaek wethout seyling samesong os un ongene un this baech wud.

Practictoid bai a woll if Closs S gurls, un dey see terns in hur ongene, blosts sund on this aise if this Furrogamo gurls und dreves awey onto this hurizin if this oshaen. This neck poir if soes see perchoses ere colled Smoll Parodime Sifts Fur Oll.

SOME GIRLS FIGHT INSIDE A BAG OF CHEETOS

Taking advantage of opacity, Girl E goes for it and punches indiscriminately. Her trembling fist, upon breaking through the flesh of another girl, transforms into words. There among the fleshy organs, she opens her fist-of-words, allowing mean, toxic syllables to thus infiltrate the body. At the point of entry, a scar is left, as a darker ring of Cheeto powder.

Girl J joins in, but also struggles with points of entry. A voice whispers that her anger is misdirected. Having been born inside this Cheeto bag, and thus covered in Cheeto powder since birth, how is she to know? At the moment of contact, Girl B, whom she is trying to hit, releases a smell. Odor or fragrance? It is unmistakably human. Girl J retracts her fist.

Girl C has done it; she has pummeled Girl G into a messy little pulp. But no. There, over there is Girl G, and this is one very beat-up little Cheeto, along with the other contents that are settling at the bottom of the bag.

RELATIONS WITH WALLS

Girl A imagines a scene vividly every morning: as the train approaches the platform, her feet at its edge, she turns away, leans her stiff and calloused back into the space between platform and train, riding the sliding surface of the train as proof of bodily friction. No wall, but wall.

Girl F stands with legs spread, arms spread wider. The wall adheres to her slightly concave body and moves with her, lateral. Self-silenced rage, a heave. Chorus of leaves: thank you. You've moved a wall.

Girl G, faced with a thick solid wall of unlovable people, is dumbfounded and takes a terrific pause before beginning to search her pockets, her purses, her crevices for anything at all that could ameliorate the situation, as if such antidotes might be tangible enough to be found in pockets, purses, crevices. Perhaps crevices.

Girl J breaks it, and breaks it, and breaks at the cost of her own body, fetishized beyond recognition. Space opens, but she has no body left to fill.

COUCH

I am capsized all day long. I fell it, we marred—break—mar again.
I entry, you execute, I return to cry and you had called it. Two eggs
in the frying pan. Everything in order, furniture. Heat too swift,
pop. Soft little tendril too late, brutal or enlightened yoke. Or both.
A bite on the terra cotta corner, brick of plastic. Where in the break.
Extinguished phone call, I give you everything anyway.

GIRLS DUCK INTO A DUMPLING TO ESCAPE THE STENCH OF SATURDAY NIGHT HUMANITY

So I count the numerous acts of procreative human copulation that contributed to this present situation: a crowd. Likewise in a stadium brimming with such by-products, all singing along to somebody else's cultural anthem.

In the dumpling we fancy ourselves protected from So Much Breeding; we are free to burn and char as we please, turning our thoughts instead to the din of the world seeping through the wrapper of the jiaozi or baozi or mandu or gyoza or har gow or bánh cuốn or ravioli or shaomai or huntun.

Girl C has her ear trained on the impending presence of an eater. Girl I knows how to exit a nightmare by punching through the wrapper. If we should be so lucky.

Time passes quickly on a Saturday night.

That arm poking out of a dumpling serves as a reminder to the world that these dumplings are yet uncooked. How now, tragic girls? What say you as the impending oil, steam, blazing pan all close in on you?

A single dumpling has the potential to be at once protein, vegetable, starch, and liquid, as articulated on its application to be officially designated an evacuation site for, you know, those cataclysmic days of the week, like today.

GIRL F IN AN OCEAN OF HATS

The waves roil and froth around the pussies as they swim, free
and proud and safe for once. Girl F, young and fit, swims hard and
fast through the acrylic, the cotton, the wool, leaving a wake of
chauvinist detritus. She can hold her own in a hot dog eating contest.
She has guts of steel, abs of steel, buns of steel, pink enamel nails
of steel. As she moves through the ocean, the hats catch on her
appendages until she becomes a roundish ball of pink. It eventually
obstructs her swimming. She rolls over and floats.

Suddenly up above is Girl D in a helicopter. Girl F waves her off. I
don't need to be rescued. I'm just resting. I'm not here to rescue you.
I'm going to take your photo for a magazine. You are exploiting me.
No I'm not. You're just jealous you didn't get to swim. Can I have
your permission to print the photo. No. I already took it. You look
gorgeous. Why don't you join me. Then no one will be able to take
the photo. Weak excuse.

Just then Girl F transforms into Girl I. Girl I strips off the hats. The
ocean grows calm. The hue of her naked body is Asian Lily White.
Black hair and pubis in sharp contrast. Girl D takes another photo.
Girl I gives permission. *Some Girls In An Ocean Of Pink.*

Just when we think we've arrived at the end of the story, the shadow of a giant figure in an oversized suit arrives and casts itself down over the entire scene. Girl A, Girl B, Girl C, Girl E, Girl G, Girl H, and Girl J arrive and form a circle. Bullets are fired into the knees of the giant figure.

It is terrifying, says Girl A.

CHARGE

てんぷくしたままの私。きりたおしたし。いりぐちの私、じっこうするアナタ、戻って眠ってもう一度泣く。フライパンで甲高い卵二個。整理整頓。迅速な熱はポンと跳ね、柔らかいつる植物は手遅れの明かりを灯す、そう。テラコッタをためしに噛んでみたら再生プラスチックのレンガでした。すべて教えてあげるから電話はここまでに。

BARTER

Girl C trades her seat on the train for the rolling eyes of Girl E,
who trades her fancy footwork for the cantaloupe toejuice I mean
dynamic invisible endgame of Girl F, who trades her future
possibility of having passagebridge for the awe-inspiring beautyjob
of Girl D, who trades her precious Klees and Mollusks and Hockneys
for all the people melting in the hot hot hand of Girl H, who trades
her firstborn son for the wild and ongoing sexual adventures of
the unassuming Girl A, who, without her wild and ongoing sexual
adventures gets on the train like she always does and finds out that
she is actually doing okay for now, things are alright as they are.

SINK OR SWIM

When the pool consists of water, only Girl F, Girl H, and Girl I are capable of lending a hand. In an ocean of people, it is Girl A who knows her way around and Girl C who will come to the rescue when you need it. In the fading light reflected off a puddle of water, Girl D contemplates her "life decisions" and determines to trade in her "husband."

DEFLATED RUBBER TURKEY

There is one atop each of the girls' heads. Clearly they have been
playing this game for a while. There is only one girl whose turkey is
still full of air, and that girl is Girl D. The game is called Duck, Duck,
Turkey. They go through the motions of having an "it," and having
that "it" walk around the outside of the circle of sitting girls, tapping
them on their turkey heads while saying, "duck, duck, duck, duck . . ."
and then they say "turkey!" while hitting the turkey on the head of a
girl and then running around the circle, trying to sit down in the
open spot in the circle before getting tagged. The general stance over
here is based on the unshakable belief that playing this game is going
to lead to a better, more just society for all, once everybody's turkey
is equally deflated. And although most of the turkeys are, indeed,
mostly deflated, none of the girls can keep themselves from glancing
furtively at the head of Girl D, her hair positively radiant in the light
bouncing off of the almost fully inflated rubber turkey on her head.
How can this be? What is wrong with everyone else's turkey? Did
Girl D get a refill? Or more air than others to begin with? Is that
really a turkey? Maybe Girl D's turkey is not made out of rubber like
the rest. What if the rubber turkey of Girl D was filled with turkey?

GIRLS RESPOND QUICKLY
TO A CALL FROM UP HIGH

The girls are minding their business—taking photos, making soup, nursing babies—when the call comes, urging them immediately to the plaza, to the bus terminal, in the middle of which stands an enormous girl, legs thick as trees, long white silk skirt billowing out in all directions.

The girls disperse under the wide hemline of the enormous girl's skirt, under which her enormous legs are planted on the ground, slightly swaying. The buses scoot around her toes as if nothing out of the ordinary.

The hair on the head of the girl up above is on fire. Her arms flail. From a distance it is uncertain whether she is dancing or drowning. As parts of her upper body threaten to detach from her lower half, the girls get to work.

Girls I and J, in their respective hemline positions, throw their weight on a piece of hem. Seated upright with their backs to the center, they unravel their long hair, sending each strand to wend its way into and upward through the weave of the silken fabric. Their hair grows and grows.

Girl G brings her posse of powerful family members, who disperse along the hemline. They each find a tear of fabric into which they sew the fabric of their own clothing. Slowly, gradually, all the colors and textures and luxuries of their own clothes dissolve into the silken fabric of the girl's skirt, forging a ballast of fabric density.

Girl D brings her crew of artists, equipped with a truck full of paints, brushes, and pigments with which they merge the colors of the plaza into the folds of the skirt. Underneath the skirt they paint the trees, the birds, the clouds—the whole forest—the legs of the girl still standing tall in their midst.

And then there is Girl B, who stares closely at the finely sewn hem of their own skirt. They look out at all the other girls throwing themselves wholly into this enormous skirt-tent operation, billowing around the City Center Plaza. Shaking off their uncertainty, Girl B takes a deep breath, then a deep squat, and they launch themself upward, stretching their body into a long, thin line, feet planted on the ground, all the way up until they are eye-to-eye with the enormous girl with her hair on fire. The girl has felt everything as it happened, felt the arrival of all the girls, the pulling and the growing and the painting on the threads of her skirt. Her feet are still solid, her soul intact, straight as a column. They converse lightly. The fire in her hair is dying out. The struggle continues, but many of these things are going to be alright.

SHAKING OR NOT

Girl G and her A-line. Bloodskirt. When the menacing shards of dried blood break in, Girl G understands it is time to stand up, flare her indignant righteous nostrils, and lift her left fist into the cleaving vastness of the sky. Right hand on right hip. Give me a G.

Girls H, I, and J huddle together a safe distance away. They keep an eye on the fist of Girl G, fiercely debating whether it is shaking or not. They keep their other eye out on the moon. They discuss the implications of both the moon and Girl G, and the impact it will have on all future actions. They note the ocean encroaching upon Girl A, also in the distance but in the other direction.

After hours of debate, they arrive at a consensus. Girl H directs the crew as they take down the moon, put the sandblaster to it, taking turns for maximum thoroughness and occupational safety. By the time the no-longer-jagged moon is replaced in the sky, the left arm of Girl G is tired from being in the air. It descends slowly, slightly. When the arm of Girl G has at last settled in its final position, the crew proceeds to cast her in bronze and raise the new monument, placing her, dubiously, in the silver medal position.

A SMALL AMOUNT OF WATER IS THROWN INTO THE SPACE BETWEEN GIRL E AND WHAT USED TO BE GIRL E

Many years of Girl E loiter inside the body of Girl E, here on the right. Facing her, on the left, inside What Used To Be Girl E, are a few years less than that.

A few pieces of candy are thrown into the space between them. Nothing happens. An arm enters the frame and offers an ice cream cone. Girl E wonders about the flavor, but nothing happens. What Used To Be Girl E starts to thin. Girl E reaches for food, though nothing is resolved.

When half of Girl E starts to die, she looks hard at What Used To Be Girl E for answers. A small amount of water is thrown into the space between Girl E and What Used To Be Girl E. The space was difficult to demarcate via candy, ice cream, or weight loss, but the water revives the colors, the surface tension connects the two bodies, and the movement of the water as it is thrown into the air and comes down and hits both girls also serves to let off steam. Now both girls can stop holding their breaths, even though the intensity of their problems is likely to persist for a while yet.

STAR CLUSTERS LIKE THE CLATTER

かたかたと in the かたか mouth of Girl か H, げん gently かた being か passed to the mouth かた of Girl か I, who then かたかたかたと turns to the なしなし pear なし skin なし lady just かた now なし reなし moving her hat かたたと. The star なし clusters かな fall かたたと out of the mouth of the pear mouth skin mouth lady mouth がたがたあら ら and into the かたたた hat, which is then かた placed かた in the mid mid middle of the なしroomなしかた. No one かた is obliがたがた gated to say anyなしanyなthing, but the かたかたからったー of clatter girls なし falls silent なし around the かたっとなしった hat.

THAT TIME WHEN GIRL F
WALKED INTO A BUBBLE BATH
WITH ALL HER CLOTHES ON

It was very beautiful.

Sometimes when we are sitting on the back porch drinking tequila mockingbirds, we remember it—and a soft smiling expression washes gently over our faces. Except for this last time it happened, everybody but me got that soft smiling expression and I alone got stuck with the resting scowl expression. One of the features of the soft smiling expression is that for the duration of one's soft smiling expression, one is unable to register any expressions on others that are not also a version of the soft smiling expression, meaning my resting scowl expression would remain invisible to everyone for as long as they kept up their soft smiling expressions. Thank goodness, because what is there to scowl at, when faced with the memory of Girl F walking into a gorgeous, vertical, geranium champagne lavender sage yarrow bubble bath with all her clothes on, just the thought of it makes me swoon, yes swoon.

_____か_____か

プールが___から成る場合，少女F，少女H，少女Iのみが___を貸すことができる。___の大海において，少女___は行き先を知っており，少女___は必要とあれば助けに来る。___たまりに映る消えゆく___の中で，少女___は「人生の___」について熟慮し「___」を下取りに出す決心をする。

1.	北極熊		16.	樺太犬
2.	沈む		17.	盆栽
3.	C		18.	B
4.	探偵		19.	決断
5.	水		20.	抱擁
6.	E		21.	I
7.	G		22.	余剰資金
8.	葡萄酒		23.	H
9.	自転車		24.	光
10.	D		25.	泳ぐ
11.	夫		26.	手
12.	人間		27.	熱帯雨林
13.	愛人		28.	A
14.	F		29.	投資
15.	革命		30.	接吻

GIRL D WITH PHOSPHORUS EYES

Exposing my wishes, I chose this poem to translate due to the word, love.

Confession. I adore the word, phosphorus. Although I may never fall in love with the girl in this poem, I love phosphorus for its own sake. This is not the task of the translator, I believe, to zero in on an isolated word such as phosphorus. My task is to serve as a custodian angel, hovering close to a girl's pulse so I can detect the heartbeat of the poet who breathed her onto the page. This poet, the lovely Sawako, and I are kindred sisters on opposite sides of this giant landmass. When she looks out the window, I am not on the other side of the ocean. Neither do I see Sawako when I walk to the end of this peninsula, where China is on the other side, a little south of Shanghai. Our mutual breath fogs the windows looking onto bodies of water that do not meet. The night rolls in as a whirling marine layer, depositing minute amounts of phosphorus in our hair and skin. We're phosphorus girls with the eyes, far too much light. A variety of phosphorus is white or red, the first in smoke-screens and flares, the latter in other flaming munitions. The heart of this dynamic equivalency is about fire and the diaphanous, but I say, it is ultimately about love. D is for diaphanous. Girl D is a diaphanous girl who is optical phosphorus.

There is no translation without love, I say to Sawako.

GIRL A JUMPS INTO THE ORCHESTRA

When my mother told me I should dress nicely, this is not exactly what any of us had in mind, because as a matter of fact, I have no nice clothes anymore, not after the last time I jumped into a new country but my things didn't make it onto the boat. It just so happens that the music was so joyful and inviting that I had no choice but to surrender to its beckon and take off all my clothes and jump in—if I had had an older brother he would have advised me against the woodwinds and the strings, telling me to jump right into the lap of a tuba player, a lap I could have made a home out of. The music cut out right in the middle of my jump as a way of letting me know I was not supposed to remove my clothes for real, that the mother I was rebelling against did not actually exist. Thanks for telling me. Out of a failure to materialize clothing mid-jump on my way to the tuba player, as recommended by my hypothetical brother, I let go of one idea after another and just decide to ride this jump wherever it takes me. By the time the curtains go up, I am wearing not only the tuba player but also the tuba. The music comes out of my buttonholes and I can see the conductor through a gap in the hair of the magnificent tuba player I now wear. I resist the urge to start dancing, which would mess up the music which would mess up the others who are already dancing to the music that they are.

UNDER THE CONDITION OF A SMALL HOLE IN THE FLOOR OF AN AUDITORIUM

Is where you will find me, sometimes in my Girl F suit, my hair as big or bigger than the rest of my body. So no that's not a rug don't you step on me. They used the word condition but that is not how I see it. They say it is a small hole but look, I am in it, and I am not a small person. An auditorium, yes. Listen. Last year I finally had my Girl F suit made which is great because now I have something to wear when under the condition of a small hole in the floor of an auditorium. We've been in many, me and the suit. And if you had hoped I would speak to the actual experience of being Girl F under the condition of a small hole in the floor of an auditorium, just remember that I am not at all Girl F, I am simply wearing a Girl F suit, and as for the questions regarding whether this is a real small hole or a small hole that is real, or a very very small real hole, and which auditorium in which circle of reality, well those questions are better resolved between you and Trisha Brown, here is her number.

SMALL WOMAN ENTERPRISING NEST AND ARROW

Outside the nest of the smallest woman in the world rests a large blazing needlearrow. On a quietly murmuring night it may appear an easy enough proposition to casually stroll by and snatch her needlearrow her big blaze and stumble quickly off with it, or to swoop down from the air and lift up and away with nary a sound, but all of that is assuming one has fully apprehended the positioning of the woman and the nest, the microgeographies of occupation, habitat, presence. Her lips a volcanic range of mountainous intention, even in sleep.

All the small women and their eyeballs. Dare them not to blink. If they don't blink, they are rewarded with a finger poke in the eye. The poker smirks. Women blink. This is how a gaze is hardened. This is how the facts escape.

Small heads of women emerge from everywhere all at once: the castle in the city, intestine of a shell, the sad well of babies lost and dead. The pigeons, the cities, the spiders arrive, and invite the small women to play. They shake them off.

步步步步步女女女女女眼眼眼眼眼

I shake them off. I am woman, stopped small gait of it too. I eye you, I you you, I fatten my eye for the sake of heat. I shape your well-intentioned hand into mine, hold tightly until we marble. The site of our marbling is both interior and exterior, which makes the timing of escape difficult to determine with precision, which was the plan all along, the long-nested night of my you, my enterprise.

I SECRETED AND WANTED TO SEE THE BEAUTIFUL SHUTTERS AT THE WINDOWS

Girl C is supposed to be hard at work today but she keeps missing her stops, slipping. As the train falls out of view once again, she returns to her world of desire, instead of the world of transport and commuting and punctuality. As soon as she allows herself to float into the passenger car, her pockets empty themselves and her clothing flies offstage as per instructions provided one hundred years ago. One hundred years ago is when the windows on the train cars used to have shutters. And beyond those beautiful shutters there used to be one hundred bells in one hundred towers. They rang to announce, all too loudly and all too regularly, the secretions of the girls floating into and out of the town.

GIRL IN A FIELD OF FLOWERS

Class, what do you see in this painting. Flowers. In the foreground or background. Both. What else. A girl. What else. Clothing. What else. An expanse of space. What else. The field of flowers flattening in the distance. Why is the field of flowers flattening. Because the painting uses one-point perspective. But what flattens them. The limits of the painter's ability to paint in extreme detail. Are the flowers in the distance the only flowers that have been flattened. Yes. No. Then what. Here are some flattened flowers in the foreground. Where. Here, not far from the clothing. What kind of clothing is that. I don't know. What else. It's crumpled. What else. I don't know. What else. It's not being worn. What do you mean. It looks like it has been taken off the body. Of whom. The girl. What makes you say that. Because the girl is naked. Why is the girl naked. Because the painting was made by a man. Are you sure. Yes. Are you sure the girl is naked. Yes. Why. Because her clothing is over there. Where. Over there. Where. Over here on the ground. Where. Over here on the ground where some of the flowers have been flattened. How do you know those are flowers. Because they are the same colors as the flowers that have not been flattened.

CLOUD PAUSE THE IRREGULAR INTERVALS AND THE DEPARTMENT OF INDEPENDENT LIGHT MANUFACTURING

More frequently in the morning. A brassy moment in the attagirl life of Girl E. Look: Girl A's hand ends up in the clouds and today returns with gestures, big slurs, a squeeze, hope.

On the escalator ride, the footwork of Girl A stages a resistance of facts. Qualifications for a regular and easy-to-anticipate use of factual matter include: vertical superiority enabling an arm to deliberate into the clouds and return with something that will bigger up without attracting attention.

Some people will never see the independent light that is too small to work its way around the bare minimum, over there in the grab bag last parking lot obstacle of death.

GIRL B ON A PIECE OF HARD GROUND

Uncrumples just in time before the light starts to fade. Trading in their light-colored clothes for dark-colored clothes, they elongate their body while someone from a distance takes aim at the space between the arch of their back, which is curved, and the surface of the ground, which is not.

The moment when that space closes is precisely the moment when the white botanica blooms in a neighboring town. An explosive purchase is made, alerting me to the ongoing need to take care of the girls.

GUN

Girl H says let's turn ourselves into bullets and load up this gun. Let's not and pretend you never said that. Come on. That way we can choose where we go and who we hit. And whose flesh we tear apart with impunity and disregard? We can reverse all the injustice by recalibrating who lives and who dies. We'll disrupt the systems through which they determine who is guilty. By turning ourselves into bullets we'll finally rid ourselves of the baggage of being female. We'll be free. We'll be powerful. We'll burn it all to the ground. You mean like when they firebombed the whole city of Tokyo. No like when you finish a board game and you start all over. We burn it all down and start again from nothing. We'll get arrested. Bullets don't get arrested. We'll be taken into the labs and analyzed they will trace our DNA then rape our mothers. Bullets don't have DNA. Bullets don't have mothers. We'll feel so guilty. Not by the time we are bullets bullets don't feel. But what if I do. What if I wuss out and jam the barrel. You don't have control over that. You said we would have control. No I didn't. We would have control.

Just then a water gun drops down from the ceiling. While the original argument carries on, the rest of the girls go bury their heads in the water.

BOARD GAME

Who is ready to begin this round. Only Girl I, who was lucky enough to have her scab fall off just this morning. It's still a little soft, but anyway she is the one who gets to go first. "Gets." "To go." "First." An elbow scab is not as big as a knee scab, but is good enough to get her firmly on the board. Until the others arrive, she has free reign on this board of dead blood. And by the time she leaves it, her detached scab will have hardened quite nicely.

Girls A through J, with the exception of Girl I, all sit taiso-style around the perimeter of the board. The game moves ahead without them, as each girl waits for her scab to fall off so that she might have a piece with which to play. There is a palpable friction in the air between those who bled specifically for this purpose and those whose injuries were of natural causes. Also for those whose scabs are soon to fall off, and those whose wounds are so fresh that they are bound to be here for a long time—they are the ones who have brought their own food, sleeping bags, and sanitary products, lest they lose their spot, or be caught elsewhere at the fateful moment when the scab comes off. There are always maybe one or two girls who have had their wounds professionally inflicted, so as to produce the largest scabs that will fall off in the briefest amount of time. Although these practices are universally frowned upon, such participants are too busy staring at their attenuated injuries to take any heed or reflect upon their misdeeds.

Sometimes there is a lull in the activity, and an old, gentle man arrives quietly with the breeze. He carries an old-fashioned epidermis knife, and asks with his eyes if anyone would like some assistance. He hums a tune. He sounds like an ice cream truck. It sounds familiar.

Over time most of the girls make it onto the board, though by the time Girl E finally makes her way there, Girl I and Girl A are already on their second scabs. Girl B explains exactly how things work around here to Girl E. Whenever a girl manages to get a scab all the way to the goal, it is a small win. The scab piece is removed from the board and thrown into a nearby pool, in fact right next to the site of the board game. This game has been going on for quite a number of years, and the pool is filling up with the used, dead, scabs of girls. Over time, each girl will get her turn to swim in the pool of discarded scabs. According to legend, the experience is quite various: some find themselves crying at the collected sufferings of girls, while others find it liberating to recall all that they have been through, as they reach the other side. Those with sensitive skin feel pricked by the jagged edges of the hard, dry scabs, whereas others find it easy enough to breaststroke their way through it all, as that is the recommended stroke for girls swimming through a pool of scabs.

PICTURE THEM, GIRLS A THROUGH J

Girl I says, don't took it me down.

Actually, all the girls talk at the same time, though they are not necessarily regarded at the same time.

A yellowy film runs down in soft folds over the right and left eyeballs of Girl D as she considers the question being asked, the specific demographics of the one doing the asking, and the potential audience for the answer. In a far corner back in the reaches of her mind, a tiny neon light starts blinking and alternating the words "audience," "recipient," "customer," and "dude." She pulls the front of her black shirt forward and sticks her face down into the darkness to consider the contours of her own body. It is too dark, though she thinks she can make out some slight movement in there, that which lies deep inside the already-debauched cavity inside of her own shirt, or can she.

WORD GETS OUT THAT
ARMS ARE FOR HUGGING

まがりかだりの心変わりのせいだったとすわガールAが振り返って抱きしめ
て痴漢をびっくりぼうてんすぐ降りる

ではなんだとガールBぐるりとひとりかいてんしたところでいったい何と何
が後ろで交差するもちあげるまちがってももちあげるなぶきぶちあけるな

ガールAも実はアームもちあげたいのにどんきほーてで買ってごらんと言わ
れてふてくさっているコでアル。きほーてしてほーきせよでアル。夏でも秋
でもおなじアツさにはかなわず、自転車にでも乗ってそよかぜを保護したら
良いといわれてなんだか情けないきぶんわるいぶききぶんアクシツコイやつ
から守りますぜさいていげん

ガールFはガールFの以前にそこでガールしたことがあるとします。そうこう
する方向方を知っているそうでござす。腕をヤサイかのように広げたコはや
はり食べる気にならない予想以上のクマのナマ腕。しかし聞いてヨそのコの
全身がこのあいだずっとひそかにこのひとときに備えていたらということで
ござす。腕と平行に口を開く。広がると平行に腕が伸びるる。そのコの口と
腕がモットもも広がったそのしゅんかんコロコロそのあかるいひとときのしゅ

んかんろろろ the moment their mouth is as wide as the widest part of their bare arms that moment is the 大 moment ロロロロ when the first person to walk into their body, that wide-open center of their body will be theirs, forever and after.

SOFT WHITE FEEL FLOWER
RUN & BLACK AIR

Girls A through J cut their tongues on the distant approaching sunlight. In the widest of waters, the cosmopolitan skies quit laughing and the shadow of the whole descends from the trees.

Bed of windows, bed of forests, bed of engines, lie down.

The pale white sky has spread completely, taking the flames for a ride around the park. That moment, I set my feelings down throughout the city, dance away the sadness.

Those who fear those who run.

GIRL E SAYING SOMETHING AS
AN ENGINE ON THE BEACH WOULD

The thickness of Girl E's silence in the process of coming to terms with the fact of being one who says something as an engine on the beach would.

She fails to communicate with precision the exact date she hopes to meet Girl K, being one who says things as an engine on the beach would.

Imagining herself to be despised and reviled by all her mortal enemies, their Ferragamo heels clicking ominously in her dreams, Girl E searches for ways to speak without saying something as an engine on the beach would.

Protected by a wall of Class S girls, one day she turns on her engine, blasts sand in the eyes of the Ferragamo girls, and drives away into the horizon of the ocean. The next pair of shoes she purchases is called Small Paradigm Shifts For All.

TEN GIRLS STEPPING INTO
AND OUT OF THE LIGHT

Girl A, always Girl A, dives headlong into her own skin as she steps into a vehicle of light, her skin rushing to catch up, enclosing her, closing her in within the steps the box she carves out the vertical column of space that is hers, the shadow closing into the vertical column that is hers, she closes it all in and holds it, holds her light vertical as if those next to her would steal it, as if Girl B in the harsh sunlight is deflecting it all away, their light, a path of shimmer in their wake, the residuals climbing near them as if the desire to remain connected a desire to be part of something, something bigger, greater than all the light a pile of girls could possibly emit. Girl C makes a go of it, moves it travels down with it, gathers it spilling over and out of her arms and Girl C uses her right elbow to turn off the light. Girl C lets in the natural. Girl C is the last one who can prevent the light from going out on that unnamed girl out there, floating, weightless, desperate, that girl who has let go, sometimes it is only Girl C that can cast a different light on the story. Sometimes when it is Girl D bringing the light, those in her charge step in or out and they remain transfixed, subjects, helpless and at the mercy of institutional sources of light, resources in and out the window, light emanating out of that window and falling right into the lap of someone seated in the same train car as Girl A, always Girl A, scooting over to make room for the delicate frame of Girl E, who never takes her shoes off, who does not yet know about the light beams that will spring forth out of her toes when finally that moment is upon us, finally that moment is here upon us finally Girl F comes in and takes charge, Girl F and Girl I they have their fingers on the light switch, we can trust their fingers on the light switch they are going to bring some light to Girl G who needs it and Girl H who doesn't need flowers but could use some money and then there is Girl J, having spent a portion of her life with her head in the sand, when she emerges, she has a ball of light in her mouth, she's never seen it before but there in her open mouth it is there.

LAKE

Like this. Luminous continuity of seeing. On one half of the space behind my back, lies. On another half of the space behind my back, multitudes of people lying down. I need to know if the cause is death or sleep or daydreaming. I wake up every person who is willing to open. It's true, there are mouths and they are full of it, but behind and from afar I can hear the marching band of hap, yeah, that old lake again, its hapful inhabitants sing, approach, and drown it all out, I insist that it does do that. And that I see you two. Even if I let go momentarily I still have an arm, even two, to fish out the meaty lies from between the layers of the water. And for each one I toss out, it most definitely rains orange petals and this is why I have been saving the whole front half of my body, the direction I am facing with all of my forward self, so that I can feel everything that is headed this way, shining heads dancing this way and that.

MOUNTAINS OF THANKS

To John Granger. Deepest respect and admiration.

*

To Keith Waldrop, Uljana Wolf & Sophie Seita, and my children for teaching me how to translate. To Shigeru Kobayashi, Jennifer Martenson, Alexis Almeida, and Komaba chiku hoikujo, for gifts of shelter and time. To Genève Chao, Hitomi Yoshio, Karen An-hwei Lee, Kyoko Yoshida, Kyongmi Park, Lynn Xu, and Miwako Ozawa, my collaborators in translation.

To Adriana X. Jacobs, Andrew Colarusso, Anna Moschovakis, Anne Waldman, Aron Aji, CAConrad, Craig Watson, Don Mee Choi, Dorothy Wang, Douglas Kearney, Erica Hunt, Erica Mena, Forrest Gander, Gabrielle Civil, George Ferrandi, Jordan Yamaji Smith, Joshua Edwards, Kaia Sand, Katrina Dodson, Madhu Kaza, Maria Damon, Naomi Kawanishi Reis, OiYan Poon, Rone Shavers, Rosmarie Waldrop, Rusty Morrison, Steven Karl, Vanessa Place, Violet Ace Harlo. To Fizz, and the ones who call me Camarada.

To my parents for letting me go, once again. To my brother for giving care. To Marina and Jona, whose play of language had huge impact on this book. To Eugene, because your love is freedom.

To Heidi Broadhead for patient and wise editing and constant support. To Joshua Beckman, Matthew Zapruder, Blyss Ervin, and Catherine Bresner. To Yoko Matoba for Japanese production assistance. To Jeff Clark for his luminous translation into book design. Especially to Jeff, Heidi, and Blyss for managing so gracefully the additional challenges of producing this book. To those who do the less visible work at Wave. To Charlie Wright, for believing in poetry.

*

To Al Filreis, Alexis Almeida, Ana Paula, C.S. Giscombe, Chris Chen, Christina Davis and Mary Graham, Dan Chelotti, E.J. Koh, Elisabeth Workman, Emily Luan, Hannah Ensor, Jen Bervin, Jen Hofer, Jennifer Firestone, Kate McIntyre, Keith Vincent, Kendall Heitzman, Lara Mimosa Montes, Leah Falk, Lillian Yvonne Bertram, Marisa Matarazzo, Michael Holtmann and Matthew Davis, Patrick Pritchett, Prageeta Sharma, Richard Henry, Ted Mathys, Teresa Carmody, Vidhu Aggarwal, Walt Hunter—and no doubt many others—for inviting me to share my work at various points in time and place.

*

Some poems have been published or are forthcoming in the following publications: *Asian American Writers' Workshop—Transpacific Literary Project, Believer Logger, Berkeley Poetry Review, Big Big Wednesday, BOMB, Carillon Street,* (『カリヨン通り』), *Colorado Review, FOLDER, HOLD, The Iowa Review, Modern Poetry in Translation, Poem-A-Day, Pulpmouth, Seedings, The Volta / They Will Sew The Blue Sail, Tokyo Poetry Journal,* and *Vestiges.*

Five poems from *Some Girls Walk Into The Country They Are From* were published as #224 in Belladonna*'s chaplet series (Fall, 2017).

"Soft White Feel Flower Run" was translated into a text-image collaboration with visual artist Naomi Kawanishi Reis between November 2017 and May 2018. The work was commissioned by Container (Jenni B. Baker and Douglas Luman) as Reel #3 of the *Look Books* subscription series, using the technology of the View-Master, a "pre-digital toy" (2018).

"Sink Or Swim" was translated and performed as part of "Asian White Feminist Performance" for *Glitch: An Evening of Poetry and Catalogue Launch* for *One Hand Clapping*, Solomon R. Guggenheim Museum (July, 2018).

"Some Girls Fight Inside A Bag Of Cheetos" and "Ten Girls In A Bag Of Potato Chips" were featured on the *The Margins—Transpacific Literary Project* on the Asian American Writers' Workshop website, together with a counter-translation of the latter poem by Tse Hao Guang (November, 2018).

"In A Plastic Bag Of Jell-O With Nine Other Girls" was published in the anthology, *The End of the World Project*, edited by Richard Lopez, John Bloomberg-Rissman, and T. C. Marshall (Moria Books, 2019).

"Girl Soup" was recorded in conversation with Katie Klocksin and Michael Slosek, published as a *PoetryNow* podcast and on the Poetry Foundation website (September, 2019).

An interview with Jordan Osborne of the *Colorado Review* about the poem "Ten Girls Stepping Into And Out Of The Light" was published together with the poem on the Colorado Review Website (December, 2019).

Six Poems From Some Girls Walk Into The Country They Are From was published as Issue #13 of *Slow Poetry In America: A Poetry Quarterly* (Spring, 2020).

I am grateful to all the editors of these above publications for their support.

CONTRIBUTOR BIOS

GENÈVE/GENEVA CHAO (pages 6, 18) was educated at Barnard College, Paris Diderot, and San Francisco State University and holds a B.A. in French (translation and literature), an M.A. in English (poetics), and an M.F.A. in Poetry. Chao has translated Gerard Cartier, Nicolas Tardy, Alain Cressan, and Christophe Tarkos and is the author of three books of poetry: *one of us is wave one of us is shore* (Otis Books|Seismicity Editions, French/English), *Hillary Is Dreaming* (Make Now Books, English), and *émigré* (Tinfish Press, English/French/guernesiais/pidgin). Chao lives in Los Angeles.

HITOMI YOSHIO (由尾 瞳, page 37) is Associate Professor of Global Japanese Literary and Cultural Studies at Waseda University. Her main area of specialization is modern and contemporary Japanese literature, with a focus on women's writing and literary communities based in Tokyo. She is also a literary translator, and her translations of Mieko Kawakami's works have appeared in *Granta*, *Freeman's*, *Words Without Borders*, *Monkey Business*, and *The Penguin Book of Japanese Short Stories*.

KAREN AN-HWEI LEE (pages 52, 76, 105) divides her time between Seattle and San Diego. She teaches in the low-residency MFA Program at Seattle Pacific University and serves as an administrator at Point Loma Nazarene University. Her recent books are *The Maze of Transparencies* (Ellipsis, 2019), *Sonata in K* (Ellipsis, 2016), and *Phyla of Joy* (Tupelo, 2012).

KYOKO YOSHIDA (吉田 恭子, pages 49, 104, 119, 135) writes fiction in English and translates from and into Japanese. Her story collections are *Disorientalism* (Vagabond) and *Spring Sleepers* (Strangers Press). Her stories appear in *BooksActually's Gold Standard 2016* (Math Paper Press), *After Coetzee: An Anthology of Animal Fictions* (Faunary Press), and others. With poet Forrest Gander, she has translated Kiwao Nomura's *Spectacle & Pigsty* (Omnidawn); with playwright Andy Bragen, *Proud Son* by Shu Matsui, *Like a Butterfly, My Nostalgia* by Masataka Matsuda, and others. She teaches American Literature at Ritsumeikan University in Kyoto.

KYONGMI PARK (ぱく きょんみ, page 42) is a second-generation Korean living and writing in Tokyo. Her collections of poetry include *Soup* (Shiyōsha, 1980), *That Little One* (Shoshi Yamada, 2003), *The Cat Comes with a Baby Cat in its Mouth* (Shoshi Yamada, 2006) and *Tales of Everywhere* (Shoshi Yamada, 2013). She has translated into Japanese *The World is Round* (1987) and *Geography and Plays*, (co-translation, 1992) by Gertrude Stein. She has participated in numerous international poetry festivals, and her work has been translated into Korean, English, Spanish, Serbian, Macedonian, Italian, and Romanian.

LYNN XU (pages 9, 26) was born in Shanghai. She is the author of *Debts & Lessons* (Omnidawn, 2013) and *June* (Corollary Press, 2006). Her poems have appeared in *6x6*, *Boston Review*, *Critical Quarterly*, *Hyperallergic*, and elsewhere, and she has performed cross-disciplinary works at the Guggenheim Museum, Sector 2337, the Renaissance Society, 300 S. Kelly Street, and Rising Tide Projects. She teaches at Columbia University and is an editor at Canarium Books.

MIWAKO OZAWA (小澤 身和子, page 82) translates from English to Japanese. Her translations include *Postcards from the End of America* by Linh Dinh, *Vagina: A Re-education* by Lynn Enright, and *Her Body and Other Parties: Stories* by Carmen Maria Machado (co-translation). She also works with Japanese and international media outlets, including BBC Radio and GQ (US), as a local fixer.

LAID OUT ALONG THE ROAD
LIKE ATTENUANT PARTS

翻訳：吉田 恭子